(

I DIDN'T
WANT
TO BE
RICH

(just enough to
re-upholster the
couch)

I DIDN'T WANT TO BE RICH

(just enough to re-upholster the couch)

Marlena Smallbone
Averyl Shilkin

ROBERT HALE • LONDON

Copyright © THIN RICH PRESS 1993.
First published in Great Britain 1994.

ISBN 0 7090 5424 6

ROBERT HALE LIMITED
Clerkenwell House
Clerkenwell Green
London EC1R 0HT

Text Marlena Smallbone

Illustrations Averyl Shilkin

Colour separations by Scott Repro Services
Designed and printed by Scott Four Colour Print
40 Short Street, Perth, Western Australia 6000

for Peter, Portia
and David
still dreaming

INVITATION

As you dance your way through life
With its ups and downs
Dip
Delve
Dive Deep
Regain your sense of fun and the fanciful
Freedom and magic
Be uplifted and dance
        FOR ISN'T LIFE
        LIKE A
        MAGIC DANCE?
This trusty companion
Will keep you warm inside
And urge you move
Into the positive . . . .

Yours artfully,

Marler x   *Averyl*

AVERYL SHILKIN

Averyl is West Australian born and after a nursing career enjoyed a ten year stint as firstly an airline hostess and then as hostess supervisor with a local domestic airline.

She was recycled as an art student graduating from Claremont School of Art. Averyl has exhibited in solo and mixed exhibitions throughout Australia and Asia. Her main interest is etching; she is a great defender of the decorative aspect of art and often finds inspiration from the literature of the "nonsense" writers.

MARLENA SMALLBONE

Marlena has degrees in Anthropology and Education. She has had an action packed life travelling with the Western Australian/All Australian Netball Team, tutoring Anthropology at University, working with gifted children and travelling the world, especially the East, studying the Buddhist Way of Life. The love of beauty and inspiring worlds of wisdom was inherited from an early age from her mother who always read fairy tales and told her that dreams do really come true.

The Cat made me buy it.

Calendar

In dwelling, be close to the land.
In meditation, delve deep into the
    heart.
In dealing with others, be gentle
    and kind.
In speech, be true.
In work, be competent.
In action, be careful of your timing.
Where there is no fight
there is no blame.

Meditations and Chinese Proverbial Wisdom

The more we care for the happiness of others, the greater our own sense of well-being becomes.

Tenzin Gyatso
The Fourteenth Dalai Lama

If one advances confidently in the direction of his dreams,
    and endeavours to live
      the life which he has imagined,
        he will meet with a success
          unexpected in common hours.

Henry David Thoreau

I feel like such a failure!
I've been shopping for over twenty
      years,
and I still don't have anything to
      wear!

                                Postcard

. . . *Be ye an island unto yourselves,*
   A refuge unto yourselves, seeking
   no external refuge.

Maha Paranibbana Sutta

When you reach the top,
You should remember to send the
    elevator
back down for the others.

Edith Piaf

If it's what you want to do you must
do it.

  . . . it will all work out.
It won't always be easy

  . . . hardly anything worth doing

   is easy.

      Beryl Markham

. . . And when she has asked me
I have tried to tell her about them . . .
But some memories I have kept for
myself as
everyone must . . .

Beryl Markham

Nothing great was ever achieved without enthusiasm.

Ralph Waldo Emerson

A Wedding in Catland

Here comes the Bride,
    With stately stride.

Louis Wain

*A Book of Verses underneath the
    Bough,
A Jug of Wine, a Loaf of Bread
    —and Thou
Beside me singing in the
    Wilderness —*

*Rubáiyát of
Omar Khayyám*

He prayeth best who loveth best
      All things great and small.

Samuel Taylor Coleridge

No man is an island, entire of itself;
every man is a piece of the continent,
a part of the main; if a clod be washed
away by the sea, Europe is the less, as well
as if a promontory were, as well as if a manor
of thy friends or of thine own were;
     any man's death
diminishes me, because I am involved in
     mankind;
and therefore never send to know for whom
     the bell tolls;
it tolls for thee.

John Donne
Devotions XVII

Wish well believe

　　　And

　　　　　Act

　　　　　　　For desire and

　　　　　　　　　Faith make dreams

　　　　　　　　　Come true.

Wishing Well

Sometimes life is filled with Banquets and bouquets.

M.S.

Look famous
Be legendary
Appear complex
Act easy
Radiate presence
Travel light
Seem a dream
Prove real.

Unknown

I'm trying to be evasive,
Don't ruin it.

Daniel Suan

Life is far too important a thing to ever talk seriously about.

Oscar Wilde

On the plains of Hesitation
bleach the bones of countless
millions who, at the dawn of victory,
sat down to wait . . .
and waiting, died.

Unknown

Happy Thought

The world is so full of a number of things,
I'm sure we should all be happy as Kings.

Robert Louis Stevenson

Face to face with the sunflower
   Cheek to cheek with the rose
      We follow a secret highway
        Hardly a traveller knows.

Unknown

Dreams are the touchstones of our characters.

Henry David Thoreau

Still the fair vision lives!
    Say nevermore
That dreams are fragile things.
    What else endures
Of all this broken world save only
    dreams!

Unknown

For Portia

The quality of mercy is not strain'd,
It droppeth as the gentle rain from
    heaven . . .
Upon the place beneath: it is twice
    bless'd:
It blesseth him that
gives, and him that takes . . .

William Shakespeare

Twinkle, Twinkle, little star,
How I wonder what you are.
Up above the world so high,
Like a diamond in the sky.
As your bright and tinsel spark,
Lights the traveller in the dark —
Though I know not who you are,
Twinkle, Twinkle, little star.

Jane Taylor

*The real voyage of discovery does not
consist in seeking new
landscapes,
but in having new eyes.*

Marcel Proust

We have to change our patterns of
　　reacting to experience.
For our problems do not lie in what
　　we experience, but in the attitude
　　we have towards it.

Akong Rimpoche

A tree as great as a man's embrace
    springs from a small shoot.
A terrace nine stories high begins
    with a pile of earth.
A journey of a thousand miles starts
    under one's feet.

Lao Tze

. . . I hadn't started out to collect diamonds but somehow they just piled upon me . . .

Mae West

*I've been rich and
I've been poor,
Rich is better.*

. . . It doesn't matter what people think of us; what matters is how we look at ourselves . . .

Yogananda

*Personal freedom is paramount
to everything.*

M.S.

The best things can't be told
    because they transcend thought.
The second best are misunderstood,
    because those are the thoughts
    that are supposed to refer to that
    which can't be thought about.
The third best are what we talk
    about.

Joseph Campbell

Times of growth

are

Beset

With difficulties

I Ching

"How do you get to Neverland?"

Second Star to the right, and
    straight
    on till morning.

J.M. Barrie

Good, Better, Best;
　　Never rest
Till "Good" be "Better"
　　And "Better" "Best".

Mother Goose

But the lark is so brimful of gladness
    and love,
The green fields below him
The blue sky above,
That he sings, and he sings; and for
    ever sings he —
I love my Love, and my Love
    loves me.

Samuel Taylor Coleridge

The two most beautiful words in the
English Language
are
"Cheque Enclosed".

Dorothy Parker

My road calls me,
Lures me,
West, East, South, North
Most men's roads lead homewards
My road leads me forth.

John Masefield

. . . Never look back. You've got to keep looking forward. Something will always happen if you try to make it happen.

Beryl Markham

*I can't stand a naked light bulb, any
more than I can stand a rude
remark or vulgar action.*

Tennessee Williams

*Oh, darling, just tell them that
wrinkled is rich*

Harry Who

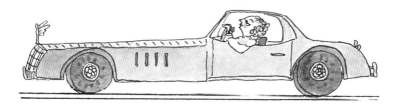

That which is most needed is
A loving heart.

Saying of the Buddha

There are few hours in life more
    agreeable than the hour dedicated
    to the ceremony known as
    afternoon tea.

Henry James

The happiness of life is made up of minute fractions — the little soon forgotten charities of a kiss or smile, a kind look, a heartfelt compliment and the countless infinitesimals of pleasurable and genial feeling.

Samuel Taylor Coleridge

Every day
  Love the beautiful,
    Seek out the true
      Wish for the good,
        And the best do!

Felix Mendelssohn

I didn't want to be rich,
I just wanted enough to get the
couch re-upholstered.

Mrs Zero Mostel

Keep cool
And collect

Mae West

If a man does not keep pace with his
    companions perhaps it is because
    he hears a different drummer.
Let him step to the music which he
    hears, however measured or far
    away.

Henry David Thoreau

. . . And hand in hand, on the edge of
the sand,
They danced by the light of the
moon.
The moon,
The moon,
They danced by the light of the
moon.

Edward Lear

Of shoes — and ships —
    and sealing-wax —
Of cabbages and kings
And why the sea is boiling hot —
And whether pigs have wings.

Lewis Carroll

Born Free
Free As the Wind Blows.

Song

Imagination is more important than knowledge.

Einstein

The finest thing in the world
Is knowing how to belong to oneself.

Michel de Montaigne

There is no duty we so much underrate
as the duty of being happy.

Robert Louis Stevenson

Where your treasure is
There your heart will be also

Matthew

A farewell is necessary before you can meet again

Richard Bach

Lullaby and Goodnight
   Let angels of light
Spread wings round your bed
   And guard you from dread
Slumber gently and deep
   In the dreamland of sleep
In the dreamland of sleep

Brahms Lullaby

A private car is not an acquired taste;
one takes to it at once . . .

Mrs Belmont

If you go down in the woods today
    You're sure of a big surprise.
If you go down in the woods today
    You'd better go in disguise
For ev'ry Bear that ever there was
    Will gather there for certain,
    because
Today's the day the Teddy Bears
    Have their picnic.

Song

Life is short but there is always time for courtesy.

Ralph Waldo Emerson

There are a thousand thoughts lying
with a man that he does not
know till he takes up his pen to
write.

William Makepeace Thackeray

What are heavy?
   Sea, sand and sorrow.
What are brief?
   Today and tomorrow.
What are frail?
   Spring blossoms and youth.
What are deep?
   The ocean and truth.

Christina Rossetti

Hold fast to dreams,
*   For if dreams die,*
Life is a broken-winged bird
*   That cannot fly.*

Langston Hughes

The Angel that presided o'er my birth
Said, "Little creature, form'd of joy
       and mirth,
Go, love without the help of
       anything on earth."

William Blake

. . . a seed of love deep in your womb
grows in the dark
and dares to bloom . . .
and so in love and peace and
warm you're born again
as your child is born . . .

Unknown

I wish I had a pretty house,
 The littlest ever seen,
With funny little red walls,
 And roof of mossy green.

Unknown

To see a world in a grain of sand
        And a heaven in a wild flower,
Hold infinity in the palm of your hand
        And eternity in an hour.

William Blake

Beloved Pan and all ye other gods who haunt this place, give me beauty in the inward soul, and may the outward and the inner man be at one.

Socrates

On this earth there is a variety of
    tastes
The sweetest of these is the taste of
    truth.

Saying of The Buddha

Secrets are your treasures
If you hand them from person
to person they become torn and
tattered.

M.S.

What I really want is to have it all . . .
Housewife, actress, mother in
manageable proportions.

Meryl Streep

A home without a cat —
      and a well-fed, well-petted and
      properly revered cat —
may be a perfect home, perhaps,
but how can it prove title?

Mark Twain

We are such stuff as
dreams are made on . . .

William Shakespeare

*Begin at the beginning . . . and go on
till you come to the end,
then stop?*

Lewis Carroll

ACKNOWLEDGEMENTS

Tenzin Gyatso, Henry David Thoreau, Maha Paranibbana Sutta, Edith Piaf, Beryl Markham, Ralph Waldo Emerson, Louis Wain, Rubáiyát of Omar Khayyám, Samuel Taylor Coleridge, John Donne, Daniel Suan, Oscar Wilde, Robert Louis Stevenson, William Shakespeare, Jane Taylor, Marcel Proust, Akong Rimpoche, Lao Tze, Mae West, Sophie Tucker, Yogananda, Joseph Campbell, I Ching, J.M. Barrie, Mother Goose, Dorothy Parker, John Masefield, Tennessee Williams, Harry Who, Henry James, Felix Mendelssohn, Mrs Zero Mostel, Edward Lear, Lewis Carroll, Einstein, Michel de Montaigne, Matthew, Richard Bach, Brahms Lullaby, Mrs Belmont, William Makepeace Thackeray, Christina Rossetti, Langston Hughes, William Blake, Socrates, Meryl Streep, Buddha, Mark Twain.